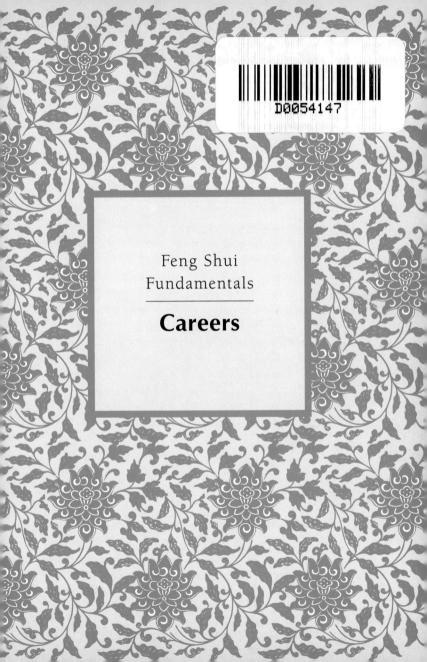

Feng Shui
Fundamentals

Careers

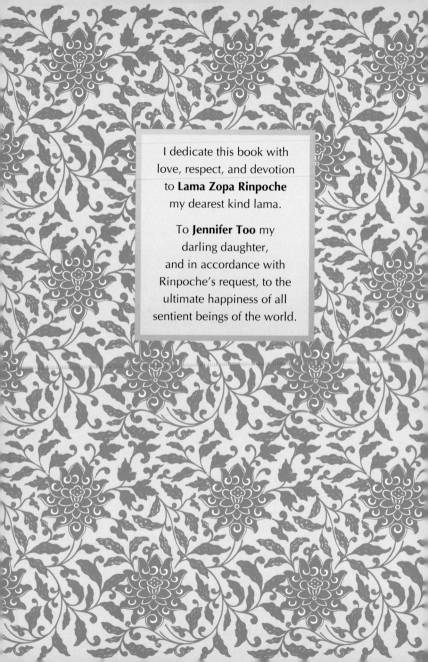

I dedicate this book with love, respect, and devotion to **Lama Zopa Rinpoche** my dearest kind lama.

To **Jennifer Too** my darling daughter, and in accordance with Rinpoche's request, to the ultimate happiness of all sentient beings of the world.

Feng Shui
Fundamentals

Careers

Lillian Too

ELEMENT

Shaftesbury, Dorset • Rockport, Massachusetts • Melbourne, Victoria

© Element Books Limited 1997
Text © Lillian Too 1997

First published in Great Britain by
ELEMENT BOOKS LIMITED
Shaftesbury, Dorset SP7 8BP

Published in the USA in 1997 by
ELEMENT BOOKS INC.
PO Box 830, Rockport, MA 01966

Published in Australia in 1997 by
ELEMENT BOOKS LIMITED
and distributed by Penguin Australia Ltd
487 Maroondah Highway, Ringwood, Victoria 3134

Designed and created with
THE BRIDGEWATER BOOK COMPANY LIMITED

ELEMENT BOOKS LIMITED
Editorial Director Julia McCutchen
Managing Editor Caro Ness
Production Director Roger Lane
Production Sarah Golden

THE BRIDGEWATER BOOK COMPANY LIMITED
Art Director Terry Jeavons
Designer James Lawrence
Managing Editor Anne Townley
Project Editor Andrew Kirk
Editor Linda Doeser
Picture Research Julia Hanson
Studio Photography Guy Ryecart
Illustrations Isabel Rayner, Andrew Kulman, Mark Jamieson,
Michaela Blunden, Paul Collicutt, Olivia Rayner, Jackie Harland

Printed and bound in Hong Kong

British Library Cataloguing in Publication Data available

Library of Congress Cataloging in Publication data available

ISBN 1 86204 119 9

The publishers wish to thank the following for the use of pictures:
Elizabeth Whiting Associates, pp 20/21; e.t. archive, p 12; Image Bank, pp 17, 23; Rex, p 19; and
Zefa, pp 7, 18, 32, 34.

Special thanks go to:
Bright Ideas, Lewes, East Sussex
for help with properties

Lillian Too's website addresses are
http://www.asiaconnect.com.my/lillian-too
http://www.dragonmagic.com

Lillian Too's email addresses are
ltoo@dragonmagic.com
ltoo@popmail.asiaconnect.com.my

CONTENTS

INTRODUCTION TO FENG SHUI

WHAT IS FENG SHUI?

風水

Feng shui is the ancient Chinese science of manipulating your living and work space to create harmonious interaction with the energies of the natural environment. Literally, the words mean "wind and water". Feng shui addresses the need to live in harmony with the earth's environment, and everything in it, artificial or natural. These intangible forces create good and bad energy or breath and herein lies the core of feng shui – the understanding of this life force or what the Chinese term "chi."

THE COSMIC BREATH

Chi can be beneficial and auspicious, bringing material benefits, well-being, and great good fortune. In this case, it is called sheng chi. But it can also be harmful and injurious – a killing breath or shar chi. Shar chi brings huge misfortune, illness, loss, and immense bad luck. Sometimes it can even result in death. Feng shui teaches us how to harness the good breath and avoid the bad.

Harnessing sheng chi involves placing objects, arranging furniture, and orienting homes and offices according to feng shui guidelines. Protecting the home from shar chi entails diagnosing arrangements and orientations that are harmful. It requires re-arranging doors and furniture to deflect this killing breath, or the use of special feng shui cures that dissolve it.

Feng shui is neither a religion nor a spiritual practice but it is multifaceted. There are elements of superstition, common sense, symbolism, and tradition in its practice, because it is a very old science, with origins as far back as 3,000 years ago. The theoretical underpinnings of feng shui are based on the Chinese view of the universe, recorded in ancient texts, some of which have survived. Feng shui is seeing a revival of interest in the closing decade of this millennium.

At the practical level, much of feng shui has come down the centuries via word of mouth, passed on from father or mother to son or daughter. This has given the practice heavily superstitious overtones that have sometimes got confused with traditional and spiritual practices. Feng shui operates on many levels and covers almost the entire spectrum of human aspiration. It can be highly personalized when practiced according to specific compass school formulas or it can be broad based and generalized. There are different schools of practice, caused as much by variations in the interpretation of ancient texts as by the differences in dialect of feng shui source books.

The feng shui methods used in this book are based on landscape form school as well as compass school formulas. The former involves interpretation of the terrain, contours, shapes, topography, elevation, rivers, and waterways, while compass feng shui uses precise measurement of geographical direction. Orientation and direction take on great significance in the practice of compass school feng shui. Neither method is more, or less, important. The approach depends on the home being investigated. In most cases, a combination of methods is used to bring about the best possible arrangement of space. It is never possible to get everything right with feng shui. Sometimes the recommendations seem conflicting and contradictory. Sometimes it is simply not possible to follow everything recommended. As long as you get the main things correct and you can generally implement 60 to 70 percent of recommendations, your feng shui can be said to be good and you can expect to benefit from the benevolent energies that will surely surround you.

This book shows the reader how feng shui can be used to improve career prospects, and there are several different and effective ways of orienting homes and offices to harness truly auspicious luck for your career.

Feng shui can be used to harness the positive energy that reinforces good career luck.

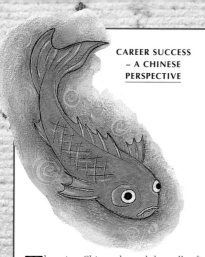

CAREER SUCCESS – A CHINESE PERSPECTIVE

There is a Chinese legend that tells of the humble carp that swims against the current up the Yellow river until it reaches the Dragon Gate, or lung men, and then, in one mighty leap, it strives to make it to the other side, successfully crossing the Dragon Gate. Those who made the leap were transformed into dragons, while those who did not would

forever bear the sign of failure, a large red dot on the forehead.

From the legend arose the belief that a dragon gate should be built to symbolize career success. These gates were usually adorned with carps that had the heads of dragons and the bodies of fish to signify their transformation to a more elevated status. It is still possible to find them in old mansions that used to belong to the most prominent mandarins in ancient China

In the days of imperial China, any scholar who passed the examinations to qualify for a powerful position at the emperor's court was likened to the carp who has ascended the Dragon Gate. Very few succeeded. Striving to ascend the Dragon Gate – deng lung men – represented the beginning of an illustrious career. Families cherished the hope that their sons would succeed, for their success meant the entire family would benefit. Scholarly success was the route to power, wealth, and great authority, for in those days, the merchant class and traders, equivalent to the entrepreneurs of today, did not enjoy the status accorded to the learned mandarins who administered the land in the name of the emperor.

Career luck in feng shui must, therefore, be seen from this perspective. It does not refer to wealth, although the attainment of a higher standard of living is always implicit in career success. Career luck means being promoted and attaining greater rank, power, authority, and ultimate influence.

Each promotion brought the mandarins of the past closer to the throne and nearer to the center of power. They can be compared to the civil servants of today, to the managers of large conglomerates, and to business magnates. Some modern corporate groupings are so large, the chief executive can, indeed, be likened to an emperor. Managers who enjoy fairly auspicious career luck can make their way to the seat of power – the board – and wield influence and authority as powerful as that exercised by the mandarins of imperial China.

Career feng shui thus brings opportunities for advancement within a bureaucracy. It leads to promotion and elevation in rank, and brings you nearer to the seat of power within your organization. However, good career feng shui also protects you against betrayal, being stabbed in the back, and being fired. In short, it ensures that you do not lose out in the cut and thrust of corporate and bureaucratic politics. Career feng shui is not concerned with acquiring wealth; it is concerned with power and influence. This does not mean prosperity is not included in the good fortune, but it is power and influence that dominate this kind of luck, not money.

This, then, is the Chinese view of career success. Who would benefit most from excellent career feng shui? The answer is politicians, civil servants, professionals, managers – in fact, anyone who holds a job and is working within a hierarchy or organization.

The legend of the Dragon Gate symbolizes career success.

THE MAIN TOOLS OF FENG SHUI

APPLYING FORM SCHOOL GUIDELINES

The practice of feng shui starts with the lay of the land, the topography that surrounds the houses or buildings in which we live. If you live in the country, this applies to mountains and hills, raised areas and plains, rivers and waterways – all the natural structures of environmental phenomena. If you live in the city, manmade structures are taken into account; buildings take the place of mountains, while roads – the arteries of the city – are likened to rivers.

Form school or landscape feng shui describes a number of classical feng shui orientations in strikingly lyrical and imaginative terms. Enormous good fortune is supposed to come to those who build their homes nestled within the embrace of the green dragon, supported by a range of hills behind (the turtle hills), and protected by a range of hills on the west (the tiger hills). In front, the land slopes to form a valley and in the distance is a small elevated hill or footstool, which signifies the phoenix. Beyond that is an auspicious view of water – a river that flows from the west

to the east or right to left. In this classical description of the ideal feng shui site, the home is facing south – in China, the source of wonderful yang energy that brings auspicious success luck. If your home is blessed with such a configuration, your family can be assured of excellent good fortune for at least five generations.

References to the green dragon, black turtle, white tiger, and crimson phoenix are purely symbolic. These are the four celestial animals that feature prominently in feng shui terminology. Homes that are sited correctly are said to enjoy the dragon's benign cosmic breath – the auspicious sheng chi that brings happiness, prosperity, health, and a large family with many descendants.

The golden rule of classical form school feng shui is mountain behind and water in front. Those who are fortunate enough to live with a view of water, and with the protection and support of mountains behind. will have excellent feng shui without even trying.

However, if the mountain is in front of you, all your ambitions and plans become blocked. So feng shui warns against having the main door open directly

IDEAL FENG SHUI POSITION

White tiger hills, placed in the west, are slightly lower than the dragon hills.

Turtle hills behind provide support.

Green dragon hills in the east are slightly higher than the tiger hills.

Water flows from right to left in front of the house like a jade belt.

Phoenix hills in the south bring opportunities.

onto a tall building or big structure. It is far better to open to an empty space, such as a park or field. If your main door is blocked by such a structure, it is advisable to re-orient it, change its direction, or use another door that is not afflicted in this fashion. If the river flows behind your home, rather than in front of it, opportunities may come your way, but you will not benefit from them.

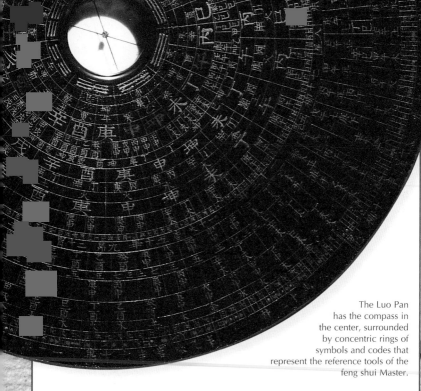

The Luo Pan
has the compass in
the center, surrounded
by concentric rings of
symbols and codes that
represent the reference tools of the
feng shui Master.

APPLYING
COMPASS SCHOOL FENG SHUI

Compass school feng shui requires the use of the compass. Traditionally, the feng shui compass, known as the Luo Pan, has been the main reference tool used by master practitioners, and many modern feng shui consultants in Asia still carry them as part of their working paraphernalia. For accuracy of readings, however, many supplement the old school compasses with more modern, Western-style compasses.

The Luo Pan has a compass in the center with the needle pointing south. This is in keeping with the Chinese tradition of placing south at the top, but in practice, this south is exactly the same as that indicated by any Western compass. The north of feng shui is therefore the magnetic north referred to in Western compass terminology. The first set of compass directions divides space into eight directions, made up of the four cardinal directions – north, south, east, and west – and four secondary directions

– southwest, southeast, northwest, and northeast. Immediately adjacent to the compass are relevant matching trigrams. There are a total of eight basic trigrams and these are arranged round the Luo Pan according to the way they are placed around the Pa Kua (see pages 14–15). These trigrams offer powerful meanings to the directions and form much of the fundamental tenets of feng shui practice.

There are then sub-directions of the eight directions. In all, the Luo Pan divides space into 24 sub-categories of directions. Thus, there are three sub-directions for every main direction. For example, south has three sub-categories of south. This is because many of the advanced formulas of feng shui require extreme accuracy when taking directions, since their potency depends entirely on precision. Then element notations and further concentric rings of other codes and symbols follow. The more advanced the feng shui practice, the larger the number of rings that are consulted.

In practical feng shui, the Luo Pan compass can be applied to a room, house, apartment, entire building, a complex of buildings, a city, and even a country. The exact codes often differ according to which Master's feng shui method is being applied, and old Masters often have their own codes and notes written on their personal Luo Pans, which they guard carefully.

For amateur practitioners, the more profound meanings of the Luo Pan are not necessary. It is sufficient to use a compass to identify the different directions of your home and to obtain your orientation. It is also necessary to understand the relationship between trigrams, elements, and directions. This approach simplifies the practice tremendously, but this does not in any way reduce its effectiveness. Indeed, these three factors form the foundation of feng shui practice. Mastering these fundamentals is, however, necessary before you can proceed to investigate the more advanced formulas.

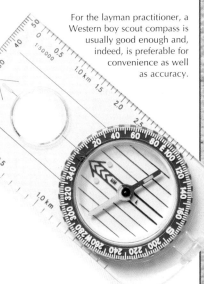

For the layman practitioner, a Western boy scout compass is usually good enough and, indeed, is preferable for convenience as well as accuracy.

THE PA KUA

The feng shui compass derives much of its meaning from the eight-sided Pa Kua symbol. Each side represents one of the eight compass directions and, in accordance with Chinese tradition, south is placed at the top. This placement is significant since the meanings and attributes of all the directions are determined from the eight trigrams placed round the Pa Kua. In feng shui it is important that the correct correlation between directions and trigrams is made. It is then possible to make progress toward the next stage, which makes reference to the five elements.

Practical feng shui requires the study of directions, trigrams, and elements – and then the interpretation and implementation of the relationships between these three important reference tools. It is only when you understand how these basic symbols of feng shui relate to each other that you can correctly put them into practice. Once these fundamentals are mastered, it becomes easier to appreciate the subtleties of compass school applications and the use of symbolic energizers.

There are two arrangements of the trigrams around the Pa Kua: The Early Heaven Arrangement and theLater Heaven Arrangement. The one shown here is the Pa Kua of the Later Heaven Arrangement, which is always used when diagnosing the feng shui of homes and buildings. Under this arrangement, the trigram that represents career success, kan, is placed in the north. This is therefore the most significant direction for those who wish to activate their career luck.

It is believed that the Lo Shu square appeared thousands of years ago on the back of a turtle, which emerged from the river Lo. This square features prominently in feng shui technology, particularly in some of the more advanced formulas.

THE LO SHU SQUARE

Another vitally important tool of feng shui is the Lo Shu square. This is a nine-sector grid, each of which contains a number from one to nine. The numbers are arranged in the grid so that the sum of any line of three, horizontally, vertically, or diagonally, is 15, the number of days it takes the moon to grow from new to full moon. The Chinese believe this is a magic square and that it provides the key that allows us to unlock many of the secrets of the Pa Kua.

The amateur practitioner should be familiar with the Lo Shu and its arrangement of numbers. Thus, since we have identified the north as the important direction to activate to achieve career luck, we can now take note that when we superimpose the Lo Shu onto the Pa Kua, the number corresponding to the direction north is one, which by itself is also believed to be an auspicious number. The Lo Shu square is also the main tool used when examining the time dimension of feng shui (see pages 52–55)

ENERGIZING THE PA KUA

Activating career luck starts with understanding the Pa Kua symbol. By itself, the Pa Kua (of the Early Heaven Arrangement) is believed to be a powerful protective tool and merely hanging it above the main door outside the home is deemed very effective in countering any negative energies that may be threatening the home and its residents. However, the Pa Kua, with its aggregated circles of meanings, is also a feng shui reference tool. There is meaning in each of the trigrams placed at every edge.

Trigrams are three-lined symbols. The lines may be solid, yang lines or broken, yin lines. The relationship of these is what gives meanings to the trigrams, according to the ancient Chinese text, the I Ching or Book of Changes.

THE DIRECTION NORTH

The trigram that represents careers is Kan and, according to the Later Heaven Arrangement of trigrams, this is placed in the north. This is therefore the corner of any home or room that represents career prospects and career luck. If this corner has good feng shui, residents will have the good fortune to attain great heights in their careers.

If this corner has bad feng shui, however, bad luck will prevail and residents will find it difficult to gain promotion or even to get a job. All avenues for advancement become blocked and they will suffer from back-biting, internal power struggles, and corporate and bureaucratic politicking. They will back the wrong person, and people will scheme against them. At its worst, bad feng shui in this corner could even lead to being made redundant or unemployed. Nothing they do will be right and no one will encourage or promote them.

Understanding the nature of career luck requires an examination of the north sector of the room or home and, in particular, the meaning of the trigram Kan.

KAN

This is probably the most dangerous of all eight trigrams. It is made up of one unbroken, yang line embraced by two broken, yin lines. This is a trigram that looks weak and yielding outside but, in fact, can be very strong inside.

Kan symbolizes the cold of winter, the danger or opportunity of water, and the cunning of the middle son. It can represent either illusions – like the moon's reflection in water – or great success through a person's ability to hide his or her strength and appear weak – the essence of cunning that is the sum and substance of this trigram.

This trigram represents situations of entanglement and a perpetual position of danger. Kan perfectly encapsulates the scenarios in ancient China when court intrigues often resulted in great danger for the mandarins who vied for promotion. One false step and death was the result;

hence this trigram represents career luck.

To enjoy a smooth and successful climb up the career ladder it is vital to activate this corner of your home and room, as well as your office. By guarding the feng shui of your north corner you will be protecting yourself from getting hurt by intrigues, deceit, and trickery. Good feng shui will ensure that sincerity of purpose is rewarded – so that the yang line sandwiched between the yin lines will stay strong and not be overcome.

PRODUCTIVE CYCLE

This illustration shows the productive cycle of the five elements - earth, metal, water, wood, and fire. Metal, the element that produces water, is in a positive position in relation to water and is therefore helping to energize water, which is associated with career success.

APPLYING ELEMENT ANALYSIS

The best method of energizing the north, thereby activating career luck, is to apply the rationale of the five elements. Every classical text on feng shui contends that all things in the universe, tangible or intangible, can be classified as one of five elements. These are fire, wood, water, metal, and earth. They are said to interact with each other in never-ending productive or destructive cycles. Element analysis must always be applied to feng shui practice and this requires a thorough understanding of how the cycles work and how they may be applied in a practical way.

THE WATER ELEMENT

The ruling element of the north is water, symbolized by anything liquid and also by water features, such as aquariums, swimming pools, lakes, fountains, and waterfalls. Identifying the relevant element to activate is a vital part of feng shui application. It suggests that placing, for instance, a swimming pool in the north part of the garden will activate excellent opportunities for career advancement. This particular type of luck is especially important for politicians, managers, professionals, civil servants, and just about everyone who holds a job in any kind of organization – whether in the private or public sectors. The two cycles that describe the elements shown here reveal various defining characteristics of the water element.

DESTRUCTIVE CYCLE

This illustration shows the destructive cycle of the five elements. Water is being overwhelmed by earth, the element that destroys water. This means that water, which is associated with career success, is not being strengthened.

▩ Water is produced by metal, so metal is said to be good for it.

▩ Water itself produces wood, so wood is said to exhaust it.

▩ Water is destroyed by earth, so earth is said to be harmful to it.

▩ Water destroys fire, so it is said to overcome fire.

From these attributes, we know that to strengthen the element of the north, we can use all objects that symbolize both the water and metal elements. Also, we should strenuously avoid anything belonging to the earth element. This means that the north may be activated by any object, color, or painting that suggests water or metal. Electrical appliances made of metal such as a television set or music center when placed in the north corner of a room, for example, are harmonious according to the five element theory. So, too, is the display of windchimes and bells, because metal creates water. Anything colored white or black is good because white represents the metal element, while black represents the water element.

It is also important to differentiate between small water and big water. A small aquarium is small water, while a river flowing by is big water. Usually small water is artificial and big water is natural. Big water is extremely potent, but it can also be overdone. How you energize the water element will depend on the particular size, shape, and orientation of your own home.

THE MAJOR SYMBOLS OF CAREER SUCCESS

ENERGIZING THE WATER ELEMENT IN THE NORTH

符號

In feng shui, each of the five elements is activated when objects that belong to the element group are present. To energize the water element of the north career corner, one of the best and easiest methods is to use small, artificial water features.

You can include water in a room in many different ways. If it is very small, an aquarium or fountain might create imbalance; in this case, all you need is a vase filled with water and flowers or a bowl of water. Any decorative item that has colored or moving water can be used to stimulate the water element. The important factor to bear in mind is never to overdo things or go overboard. If you create a large artificial water feature in your living room, for instance, it might look very spectacular, but it will overwhelm all the other energies. Instead of activating the element, the water will drown you, causing you to suffer all the negative consequences of poor feng shui.

However, you should note that while the water corner can be activated effectively to enhance careers, this should be confined to your living room or office. Fountains and aquariums should never be placed in the bedroom. Feng shui tradition states that an aquarium that is placed behind your bed may cause you to be robbed or cheated.

If you can afford it, install a small water fountain against the north side of your living room wall. There are many different designs available and all that is needed is a small pump to create a continuous flow of water.

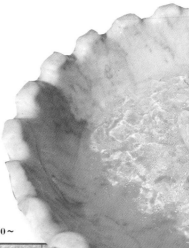

An aquarium makes an excellent water energizer. Fish swimming about and an oxygenator creating bubbles ensure the water is moving. Stagnant water creates stagnant chi and this is worse than not having water at all. Place a light above the aquarium, as this creates the movement of shadows on the ceiling.

WATER MOTIFS AND COLORS

These can be incorporated into the overall interior design of your living room. Make them look esthetically pleasing. The colors of the north sector are black or any shade of blue to reflect the water element. Incorporate this color scheme into wallpaper, drapes, and rugs. The north wall itself can also be painted in any shade of blue. Lighting in this corner should be subdued.

As a rule, feng shui Masters usually advise against having a swimming pool in the home. This is not because it is inauspicious, but simply because if you place it in the wrong sector of your plot, its shape is wrong, or its size creates massive imbalance, it is likely to do a great deal of harm to residents. It is very easy to get swimming pools wrong.

A swimming pool in the grounds of a large house, however, can bring extremely beneficial energies if everything is done right. It must be placed correctly, fashioned in an auspicious shape, and its size should balance both the house or building and the grounds.

Locate a swimming pool in the north, east, or southeast of your grounds. It can be extremely harmful and cause

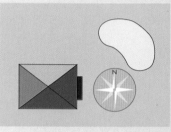

If this pool is in the north corner of your land, the location is acceptable and can be auspicious. However, if from inside the house looking out, it is on the right-hand side of the main door, this could cause strife in the relationship of residents. Also the pool is too large for the size of the house and is too near it. Swimming pools have to be very carefully planned.

Kidney-shaped or circular pools are auspicious. Best of all, is to allow the pool to embrace the home.

problems if it is located in the south. It is also more auspicious when it is in a position where it can be seen from the main door. For women, the advice is that a swimming pool should never be on the right of the main door (seen from the inside looking out). If it is on the right, a husband will develop a roving eye and become unfaithful.

Round and circular shapes are considered superior to rectangular pools with pointed corners. The best shape is kidney-shaped or like a double eight; one whereby the pool seems to be embracing the house. When a house is embraced by water, especially water that appears to come from the north, it is an excellent feng shui feature.

If you have a swimming pool on your land, ensure that it is visible from at least one of the doors of the home. It is also vital that the water is kept clean. There is nothing more damaging to the feng shui of a home than a body of dirty and polluted water. This allows the precious chi to become stale and harmful, causing the home's residents to suffer from ill health and loss. There can be no career luck when this happens.

ENERGIZING THE TURTLE

A small pond with a live turtle or terrapin is better than a swimming pool. In fact, if you want to make certain you will never be lacking in support in your job, you should symbolically invite the celestial turtle into your home. If a terrapin pond in the north side of your garden is impractical or if you live in an apartment, buy a ceramic turtle and place it in a bowl of water in the north corner of your home or living room. This is one of the easiest and most effective methods of energizing excellent career feng shui. You will never lack support and it will create a great deal of goodwill and respect for you at the office. The turtle is also a symbol of longevity and having him in the home energizes health as well. Keep only one turtle (or terrapin) since the lucky number of the north is one.

The turtle is a symbol of career support, as well as longevity.

SYMBOLS OF THE METAL ELEMENT

The Chinese word for metal also means gold. In feng shui, gold does not just represent money. It is also the symbol of prominence and affluence. Symbols that stimulate this element when placed in the career corner are believed to bring great success to those engaged in public life.

INSIGNIA OF RANK

In the old days of imperial China, court mandarins wore robes embroidered with insignia to signify their rank. Nowadays, wealthy Chinese collect well-preserved antique robes that have their insignia intact to hang in their homes. They are thought to produce an auspicious aura in which the cosmic currents can generate favorable good luck that leads to elevation in rank. Other decorations and success symbols can be used for the same purpose.

COINS

Coins can be really effective for activating the north corner. For this purpose it would be excellent to use old Chinese coins with a square hole in the center, but it would be easier to use the ordinary coins you find in your small change. Set aside a small, decorative box, preferably one that is made of metal – brass, pewter, or silver – and keep all your leftover change inside. Place this box anywhere in the north corner. A variation on this idea is to use an antique metal bowl containing leftover coins.

Coins will stimulate the metal element and encourage career luck if they are placed in the north corner.

MAGNET

Horseshoe-shaped magnets are universal good-fortune symbols. Place one on the floor, under or inside a cupboard. This symbolizes gold hidden within and is believed to symbolize good luck.

BELL

Bells are very symbolic of high position. If you are hankering after a promotion, get a small silver- or gold-colored bell and hang it on a wall in the south or you can place a dinner bell on the south side of the dining room to activate the good luck of that corner each time you sit down for supper.

WIND CHIMES

These have several uses in feng shui since they are believed to be effective cures to dissolve the negative influence of beams and sharp-edged corners. Hung in the north, they are also excellent for attracting auspicious chi that creates good fortune for those who wish to advance in their careers.

Windchimes placed in the north should be made of metal and the rods should be hollow. This allows the chi to be channeled to the corner. Windchimes with solid rods have no feng shui significance. The number of rods in the windchime should ideally be one of the good luck numbers – one, six, seven, or eight. It is not advisable to hang windchimes that have five rods.

INDIVIDUAL CAREER ORIENTATIONS

YOUR SELF-DEVELOPMENT
CAREER DIRECTION

方
位

You can calculate the direction that is the most auspicious for your career, based on an old and very powerful compass school formula. This formula uses your date of birth and the exact method was for many years a closely guarded secret. Known as the Pa Kua Lo Shu formula (or Kua formula), it was given to the author's feng shui Master by an old Taiwan feng shui Grand Master. The formula was derived from the two ancient symbols of feng shui – the eight-sided Pa Kua, with its many levels of meanings, and the Lo Shu magic square, a nine-sector grid that is believed to be the key to unlocking the secrets of the Pa Kua.

According to the feng shui Masters, each person has four auspicious and four inauspicious directions, depending on whether he or she is an east or west group person. What group you belong to is determined by your year of birth and gender.

The auspicious career direction of every person is known as the fu wei direction. Once you know your personal fu wei direction, you can make use of that information in many different ways to enhance your personal feng shui. You can use it with equal success in your home, as well as in the office. Essentially this means sleeping and sitting in a direction that allows you to capture your fu wei. Capturing the luck of your direction implies

If your Kua number is:
1 east group
2 west group
3 east group
4 east group
5 west group
6 west group
7 west group
8 west group
9 east group

embarking on a career path that leads to phenomenal success within your chosen profession. You will feel capable and energized at work and really start to enjoy being there. You will catch the eye of your manager and promotion will seem a foregone conclusion.

This formula is most suitable for people who are interested in pursuing a career and who have ambitions to climb to the very top. It is not for enhancing income, as much as for personal growth and development, but implicit in good career luck is a significant improvement in your standard of living.

Your Career orientation is:

NORTH for both males and females

SOUTHWEST for both males and females

EAST for both males and females

SOUTHEAST for both males and females

SOUTHWEST for males and
NORTHEAST for females

NORTHWEST for both males and females

WEST for both males and females

NORTHEAST for both males and females

SOUTH for both males and females

THE KUA FORMULA

Calculate your Kua number as follows. Add the last two digits of your Chinese year of birth. e.g. **1948**, **4+8=12**
If the sum is higher than ten, reduce to a single digit, thus **1+2=3**

Males	Females
Subtract from	Add
10	**5**
thus	thus
10-3	**5+3**
=7	**=8**
So, for men born in	So, for women born in
1948	**1948**
the Kua number is	the Kua number is
7	**8**

Now check against this table for your family direction and location.

THE KUA FORMULA

To determine your career orientation, first determine your Kua number. Obtain your Chinese year of birth based on the calendar on pages 28–29 and use this calculation to get your Kua number.

THE CHINESE CALENDAR

Note that for the Chinese, the New Year begins in either late January or early February. Take note of this when calculating your Kua number. Thus, if you were born in January 1946 before the New Year, your Chinese year of birth is said to be 1945 and not 1946. This calendar also indicates the ruling element of your year of birth. This gives you further clues on which corner of the home, will have the most effect on your well-being.

Year	From	To	Element	Year	From	To	Element
1900	31 Jan 1900	18 Feb 1901	Metal	1923	16 Feb 1923	4 Feb 1924	Water
1901	19 Feb 1901	17 Feb 1902	Metal	1924	5 Feb 1924	24 Jan 1925	Wood
1902	18 Feb 1902	28 Jan 1903	Water	1925	25 Jan 1925	12 Feb 1926	Wood
1903	29 Jan 1903	15 Jan 1904	Water	1926	13 Feb 1926	1 Feb 1927	Fire
1904	16 Feb 1904	3 Feb 1905	Wood	1927	2 Feb 1927	22 Jan 1928	Fire
1905	4 Feb 1905	24 Jan 1906	Wood	1928	23 Jan 1928	9 Feb 1929	Earth
1906	25 Jan 1906	12 Feb 1907	Fire	1929	10 Feb 1929	29 Jan 1930	Earth
1907	13 Feb 1907	1 Feb 1908	Fire	1930	30 Jan 1930	16 Feb 1931	Metal
1908	2 Feb 1908	21 Jan 1909	Earth	1931	17 Feb 1931	15 Feb 1932	Metal
1909	22 Jan 1909	9 Feb 1910	Earth	1932	16 Feb 1932	25 Jan 1933	Water
1910	10 Feb 1910	29 Jan 1911	Metal	1933	26 Jan 1933	13 Feb 1934	Water
1911	30 Jan 1911	17 Feb 1912	Metal	1934	14 Feb 1934	3 Feb 1935	Wood
1912	18 Feb 1912	25 Feb 1913	Water	1935	4 Feb 1935	23 Jan 1936	Wood
1913	26 Feb 1913	25 Jan 1914	Water	1936	24 Jan 1936	10 Feb 1937	Fire
1914	26 Jan 1914	13 Feb 1915	Wood	1937	11 Feb 1937	30 Jan 1938	Fire
1915	14 Feb 1915	2 Feb 1916	Wood	1938	31 Jan 1938	18 Feb 1939	Earth
1916	3 Feb 1916	22 Jan 1917	Fire	1939	19 Feb 1939	7 Feb 1940	Earth
1917	23 Jan 1917	10 Feb 1918	Fire	1940	8 Feb 1940	26 Jan 1941	Metal
1918	11 Feb 1918	31 Jan 1919	Earth	1941	27 Jan 1941	14 Feb 1942	Metal
1919	1 Feb 1919	19 Feb 1920	Earth	1942	15 Feb 1942	24 Feb 1943	Water
1920	20 Feb 1920	7 Feb 1921	Metal	1943	25 Feb 1943	24 Jan 1944	Water
1921	8 Feb 1921	27 Jan 1922	Metal	1944	25 Jan 1944	12 Feb 1945	Wood
1922	28 Jan 1922	15 Feb 1923	Water	1945	13 Feb 1945	1 Feb 1946	Wood

Year	From	To	Element	Year	From	To	Element
1946	2 Feb 1946	21 Jan 1947	Fire	1977	18 Feb 1977	6 Feb 1978	Fire
1947	22 Jan 1947	9 Feb 1948	Fire	1978	7 Feb 1978	27 Jan 1979	Earth
1948	10 Feb 1948	28 Jan 1949	Earth	1979	28 Jan 1979	15 Feb 1980	Earth
1949	29 Jan 1949	16 Feb 1950	Earth	1980	16 Feb 1980	4 Feb 1981	Metal
1950	17 Feb 1950	5 Feb 1951	Metal	1981	5 Feb 1981	24 Jan 1982	Metal
1951	6 Feb 1951	26 Jan 1952	Metal	1982	25 Jan 1982	12 Feb 1983	Water
1952	27 Jan 1952	13 Feb 1953	Water	1983	13 Feb 1983	1 Feb 1984	Water
1953	14 Feb 1953	2 Feb 1954	Water	1984	2 Feb 1984	19 Feb 1985	Wood
1954	3 Feb 1954	23 Jan 1955	Wood	1985	20 Feb 1985	8 Feb 1986	Wood
1955	24 Jan 1955	11 Feb 1956	Wood	1986	9 Feb 1986	28 Jan 1987	Fire
1956	12 Feb 1956	30 Jan 1957	Fire	1987	29 Jan 1987	16 Feb 1988	Fire
1957	31 Jan 1957	17 Feb 1958	Fire	1988	17 Feb 1988	5 Feb 1989	Earth
1958	18 Feb 1958	7 Feb 1959	Earth	1989	6 Feb 1989	26 Jan 1990	Earth
1959	8 Feb 1959	27 Jan 1960	Earth	1990	27 Jan 1990	14 Feb 1991	Metal
1960	28 Jan 1960	14 Feb 1961	Metal	1991	15 Feb 1991	3 Feb 1992	Metal
1961	15 Feb 1961	4 Feb 1962	Metal	1992	4 Feb 1992	22 Jan 1993	Water
1962	5 Feb 1962	24 Jan 1963	Water	1993	23 Jan 1993	9 Feb 1994	Water
1963	25 Jan 1963	12 Feb 1964	Water	1994	10 Feb 1994	30 Jan 1995	Wood
1964	13 Feb 1964	1 Feb 1965	Wood	1995	31 Jan 1995	18 Feb 1996	Wood
1965	2 Feb 1965	20 Jan 1966	Wood	1996	19 Feb 1996	7 Feb 1997	Fire
1966	21 Jan 1966	8 Feb 1967	Fire	1997	8 Feb 1997	27 Jan 1998	Fire
1967	9 Feb 1967	29 Jan 1968	Fire	1998	28 Jan 1998	15 Feb 1999	Earth
1968	30 Jan 1968	16 Feb 1969	Earth	1999	16 Feb 1999	4 Feb 2000	Earth
1969	17 Feb 1969	5 Feb 1970	Earth	2000	5 Feb 2000	23 Jan 2001	Metal
1970	6 Feb 1970	26 Jan 1971	Metal	2001	24 Jan 2001	11 Feb 2002	Metal
1971	27 Jan 1971	15 Feb 1972	Metal	2002	12 Feb 2002	31 Jan 2003	Water
1972	16 Feb 1972	22 Feb 1973	Water	2003	1 Feb 2003	21 Jan 2004	Water
1973	23 Jan 1973	22 Jan 1974	Water	2004	22 Jan 2004	8 Feb 2005	Wood
1974	23 Jan 1974	10 Feb 1975	Wood	2005	9 Feb 2005	28 Jan 2006	Wood
1975	11 Feb 1975	30 Jan 1976	Wood	2006	29 Jan 2006	17 Feb 2007	Fire
1976	31 Jan 1976	17 Feb 1977	Fire	2007	18 Feb 2007	6 Feb 2008	Fire

HOW TO APPLY THE FORMULA

The home or office layout should be demarcated into the nine sectors according to the Lo Shu grid as shown. To do this accurately, use a good measuring tape and try to get the demarcations as accurate as possible.

Next get your bearings and identify the eight corners according to the compass directions of each. Use a good compass (any Western compass will do) and, standing in the center of the home or office, identify the nine locations by dividing the total floor space into nine equal grids. Draw out the floor plan of the home or office being investigated, as this will greatly assist you in arranging your rooms and furniture. This method of

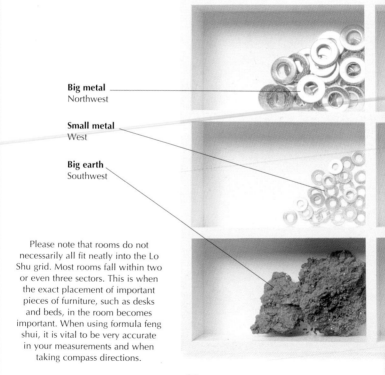

Big metal
Northwest

Small metal
West

Big earth
Southwest

Please note that rooms do not necessarily all fit neatly into the Lo Shu grid. Most rooms fall within two or even three sectors. This is when the exact placement of important pieces of furniture, such as desks and beds, in the room becomes important. When using formula feng shui, it is vital to be very accurate in your measurements and when taking compass directions.

demarcating the home according to the Lo Shu square is an excellent way of identifying the corners of the home.

Even as you identify the sectors of the home or office, keep their matching elements at the back of your mind. This is because the application of the five element theory transcends every school of feng shui and irrespective of the method or formula that you are using, it is necessary to remember this. For ease of reference, the relevant elements are indicated in each of the sectors. This is according to the Later Heaven Arrangement of the trigrams, the Pa Kua arrangement that is always used in feng shui for the homes of the living. The element of the center is earth.

Water
North

Fire
South

Earth
Northeast

Big wood
East

Small wood
Southeast

Applying the Kua formula so that your energies are in a positive relationship with your living and working space will help to ensure a successful and fulfilling career.

APPLYING THE KUA FORMULA

Once you know your personal career direction and you have demarcated your floor area according to the Lo Shu square, there are several ways you can start to match your individual chi energies with that of your environment, thus activating your directions and attracting auspicious sheng chi for your personal benefit.

Your Kua number from the table on page 27 offers you your most auspicious direction for ensuring that you will be more than up to your job or profession. It also identifies your luckiest compass location for your main doors, office,

bedroom, and study to ensure your career luck stays smooth and that you do not succumh to the stresses and strains of working life. Incorporating this formula into your personal feng shui is also a very effective safeguard against losing out in any power struggle at the office. People you work for will have more respect for you, while people who report to you will stay loyal.

The luck referred to here is best activated for each member of the family according to each person's most suitable direction and location, as indicated in the Kua table.

YOUR DOORS
AND IMPORTANT ROOMS

Perhaps the best way of capturing good career luck through the use of this method is to try to match all your most important doors according to your best career location and to try to work, sitting in and directly facing your career direction. This means locating these important rooms and doors in the sector that is the luckiest for you. It also means that you place your furniture in such a way that you are working and sleeping according to your luckiest direction.

EXAMPLE

If your career direction is north, for instance, the diagram shows where your main door, bedroom, or office should be located and in what direction your main door should be facing.

This is the north corner of the home according to the compass and would be the ideal location for all your most important rooms. If the door coming into the room is also facing north (as shown), it would be perfect, but in reality this is seldom possible. So tap either the direction or the location. Do not worry if you cannot get both right.

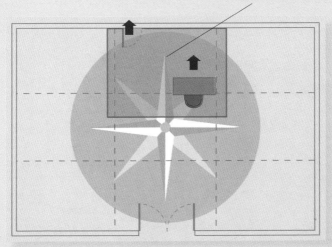

Try to have the main door face your career direction. If you cannot, then let it face one of your four good directions.

IRREGULAR-SHAPED HOME AND OFFICE LAYOUTS

Homes and offices seldom have regular, square, or rectangular shapes, making it difficult to superimpose a nine-sector grid onto the floor layout. More serious is the problem of missing corners. If your career corner is missing as a result of the shape of your home or, worse still, your office, then your career luck could be seriously undermined.

There are ways of getting round this problem and these are shown here, but correcting the problem merely improves the situation. It does not create the good career luck you would want.

According to feng shui, missing corners mean the home will be lacking in certain luck aspects. What types of luck are missing depend on the corresponding

THE WORKING DIRECTION

This is one of the most vital determinants of good career luck. Try to work sitting and facing your personal best direction for activating this aspect of your luck. It is a good idea actually to draw an arrow on your desk to remind you to face this direction when meeting people, working on a project, or using your computer.

Building an extension is the best cure, but this depends on the space available.

compass directions of missing sectors. If one missing sector represents your career direction, you can partially correct the matter by one of the following methods.

▨ Install a light.
▨ Hang a wall mirror.
▨ Build an extension.

What you do depends on your circumstances and whether you have the space.

An irregular-shaped layout sometimes makes it difficult to have the working office or desk located in your best corner. If you cannot get the location you need, tapping the career direction is often good enough. This means you work facing your best direction. If you cannot tap either the location or the direction, do try to work facing at least one of your three other auspicious directions.

A mirror on the wall extends it outward, thereby correcting the problem.

A light corrects the problem.

EAST AND WEST GROUP DIRECTIONS

Compass feng shui divides people into either east or west group people. Each person is said to have four favorable directions, with each one representing a different kind of auspicious luck. In addition to your career and personal-development direction, therefore, you will have three other auspicious directions. All these favorable directions belong to the same east or west group.

What group you belong to depends on your Kua number.

.

East group people have Kua numbers one, three, four, and nine. East group directions are east, north, south, and southeast.

.

West group people have Kua numbers two, six, seven, and eight. The west group directions are west, southwest, northwest and northeast.

East group directions are inauspicious for west group people and west group directions are harmful for east group people! This is equally true for locations.

KUA NUMBER
east/west group

1	east group
2	west group
3	east group
4	east group
5	west group for males
5	west group for females
6	west group
7	west group
8	west group
9	east group

INAUSPICIOUS DIRECTIONS

The compass formula also tells you the directions that will hurt you. These four bad directions are different for each of the Kua numbers and they vary in the intensity of bad luck they bring.

▨ The Ho Hai direction puts all the blame on your shoulders! You will be the eternal scapegoat.

▨ The Wu Kwei direction brings five ghosts to your doorstep. Enemies will harm you.

▨ The Lui Shar direction attacks you with six killings. You are plagued with bad luck at every step.

▨ The Chueh Mung direction is the most severe, meaning total loss.

Ho Hai direction	Wu Kwei direction	Lui Shar direction	Chueh Ming direction
West	Northeast	Northwest	Southwest
East	Southeast	South	North
Southwest	Northwest	Northeast	West
Northwest	Southwest	West	Northeast
East	Southeast	South	North
South	North	East	Southeast
Southeast	East	North	South
North	South	Southeast	East
South	North	East	Southeast
Northeast	West	Southwest	Northwest

YOUR UNLUCKY DIRECTIONS

SE	S	SW
E		W
NE*	N	NW

It is important to remember your unlucky directions, especially when orienting your main front door and the door to your office, and your sitting, working, and sleeping directions.

Try drawing out your personalized Kua chart as shown. For example, if your Kua

number is eight, your Kua chart will look like this, with the inauspicious directions marked in blue, the career direction starred, and the auspicious directions marked in red.

The table shows you the four harmful directions according to your Kua number.

ENERGIZING CAREER LUCK IN THE HOME

THE MAIN DOOR

Irrespective of what kind of luck you want, the feng shui of your main door plays a big part in determining whether you get it. Auspicious luck comes to those who are able to locate and orient the main door to their homes according to their personal auspicious compass directions. It is, however, also necessary to protect the main door from being hit by shar chi created by offensive structures outside and inside the home. There should be nothing sharp, straight, or angular, that seems to be

1

House number 1 is being hit by the straight road. This T junction configuration is very dangerous and should be avoided.

2

House number 2 is being hit by the dead tree across the road, again a most inauspicious feature. Try to have the tree cut down or re-orient your door.

3

House number 3 is being affected by the supermarket building, but since it is some distance away, it is not very harmful.

4

House number 4 is being hit by the statue in the park. The energy from the statue would be even more harmful if the man on horseback directly faced the horse.

aimed directly at the main door. These create what is termed secret poison arrows that cause misfortune to befall the residents, even when the door orientation has been auspiciously arranged.

Poison arrows are a powerful source of the killing breath. The most common of these harmful structures are straight roads, overpasses, trees, and buildings, but it is necessary to be alert to other, not so obvious structures, which can also represent poison arrows. Remember that nothing massive should be threatening your door.

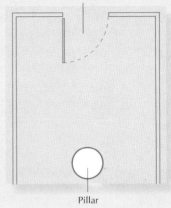

INSIDE

Main door

Pillar

If a main door directly faces a pillar inside the house, it is a major problem. It is advisable to re-locate it.

On the inside, take care that the main door is not directly facing a pillar, a mirror, the door to the toilet, or opposite another door. These are all very harmful situations. Finally, do not site it directly below a toilet on the upper floor. This causes harmful shar chi to attack it from above.

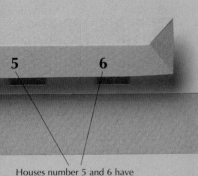

5   **6**

Houses number 5 and 6 have better feng shui. House 6 is the best, since there is nothing blocking its main door. In front is the park, which represents what feng shui terms the auspicious bright hall where benign good-fortune chi accumulates and settles before entering the home.

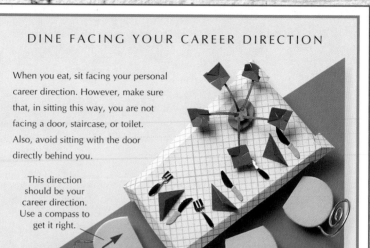

DINE FACING YOUR CAREER DIRECTION

When you eat, sit facing your personal career direction. However, make sure that, in sitting this way, you are not facing a door, staircase, or toilet. Also, avoid sitting with the door directly behind you.

This direction should be your career direction. Use a compass to get it right.

GETTING THE OVEN "MOUTH" RIGHT

Another important feature in the home that affects career success is the way in which your food is cooked. Feng shui argues that to tap good career luck, the cooker or oven should be cooking your food with energy that is coming from your most auspicious career direction. Hence it is necessary to arrange your oven in such a way that the electrical cord or gas supply entering the oven is coming from your career direction.

If your most auspicious direction is south, then your cooker should be connected to its power source on the south wall.

The Chinese use the rice cooker to get this right and this is, of course, a lot easier than trying to move the oven around. However, the rice cooker works only because rice is the staple food of the Chinese. If all you ever eat is buttered toast, you could use the toaster to meet this particular requirement.

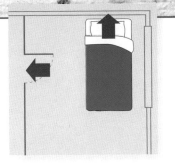

The bed is placed between the door and the window, a very inauspicious arrangement. You cannot benefit from a such a sleeping orientation.

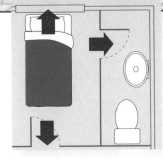

The bed is placed under a window. This is not recommended and should be avoided. The door of the toilet is also too close to the bed. Keep the toilet door closed.

TAP YOUR CAREER LUCK
WHILE YOU SLEEP

Arrange your bed so that your head is pointed in your career direction. The sleeping direction is one of the most important applications of the Kua formula. However, you must also make sure you observe some simple feng shui guidelines as well. Do not sleep with your feet or your head pointed directly at the door or the toilet. You should not sleep under a beam or with a corner edge hitting at you. All these features cause you bad luck and can nullify all your other efforts. The ideal place for your bed is diagonally opposite the entrance door. Meanwhile, also check the direction of the door into your bedroom. If it faces one of your good directions, it is auspicious for you. However, this is something you can compromise on. It is most important to sleep in your career direction.

The bed is placed with the feet pointed at the door. This is called the death position and will cause extreme ill health or loss. Also the corner edge is sending poison arrows at the sleeper.

The bed is placed directly under an overhead beam, which will cause headaches and insomnia. Move the bed out of the way. There is a mirror directly facing the bed. This, too, is bad – remove it.

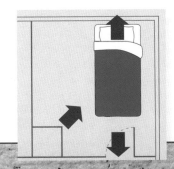

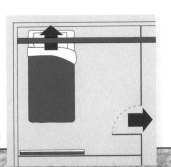

COLUMNS AND PILLARS

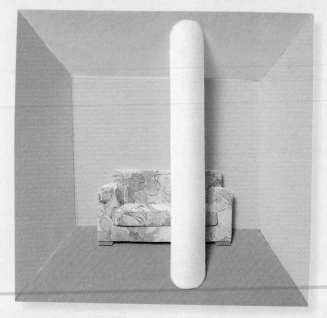

OTHER FENG SHUI HAZARDS INSIDE THE HOME

Unless you live in a huge house, columns and pillars inside the home are really bad news, simply because they overwhelm the home and create massive disharmony, especially when they are square and stand alone. Round pillars do less harm because they do not have the harmful edges of square pillars.

Imagine sitting with a column confronting you each day. Many homes have such features, which are the result of poor architectural and structural design. If you have columns in your home, do one of the following things.

▧ Wrap the column round with mirrors. This will effectively make the column disappear.

▧ Place potted plants to cover the edges of the columns.

▧ Hang a wind chime from the top of the edge of the column.

Hanging two bamboo flutes, with the playing side down in this way, is also very effective in countering the shar chi of overhead beams.

Windchimes are a popular and effective way of countering the bad feng shui of beams, but do check the elements.

EXPOSED OVERHEAD BEAMS

Feng shui explains that there should never be anything threatening or foul above you. These features will press down on your inner life force and cause you severe heartache and illness, not to mention extreme bad luck. Beams are, of course, always present in a home, but the less exposed they are, the better. All furniture should be arranged with an eye to any exposed beams that you may have.

Do not sit, sleep, eat, or work with a beam directly above you. There is no feng shui cure except to move your chairs and beds out of the way. Ideally, exposed beams should be camouflaged with a false ceiling. If this is not possible, the quick solution is to hang a windchime, provided the beam is not in the east or southeast of the room. Another popular method is to hang two bamboo flutes, activated with red string, diagonally to each other.

FENG SHUI AT THE OFFICE

ENERGIZING CAREER LUCK AT WORK

工作间

Career luck from feng shui is available to everyone. The beauty of the Kua compass formula method is that anyone can use it, since it is easy enough to orient your personal sitting direction at work. All you need do is think about the immediate space surrounding you. Whether you are a humble clerk or a powerful chief executive, if you work facing your personal career direction, you will benefit from excellent compass feng shui.

Problems arise when the office that adjoins yours blocks your luck, or when there are annoying protruding corners, overhead beams, and huge columns in your office that you cannot remove. However, if you know some of the basic principles of feng shui, you will become aware of furniture, structures, and arrangements that will be inauspicious for you. In most cases, you can do something to reduce or completely dissolve the negative effects you might otherwise be subjected to.

Offices should not be irregular in shape. Tight spaces and sharp corners should be strenuously avoided if possible. It is better to have a smaller space that is regular in shape!

Never sit behind a door or a window. When you sit with the window behind you, you will be lacking in support. When you sit with the door behind you, you will be stabbed in the back.

LOCATION OF YOUR OFFICE

If you are lucky enough to have a private room, it will be most auspicious if it is located deep inside the office, diagonally opposite the entrance. If you are the manager, always try to get this room or alternatively go for the room that is located in your personal career direction. Try to avoid working in an office at the end of a long corridor, too near the entrance door, or facing a staircase or toilet.

PLACEMENT OF THE DESK

Inside a room, the best place for the desk is the corner opposite the door. However, there are certain arrangements that are especially harmful to your well-being and your career luck.

To simulate the support of a mountain behind you, hang a painting or a print of a range of mountains that resemble turtle hills. A picture of a large turtle is also a great idea.

Sitting with the window behind is never recommended. It indicates a sad lack of support for you and your work. However, if the view shows a range of hills in the distance, the effect is most auspicious.
If the view behind you is that of a big building, such as a bank head office, then it is equally auspicious. It means that there is something solid behind you.

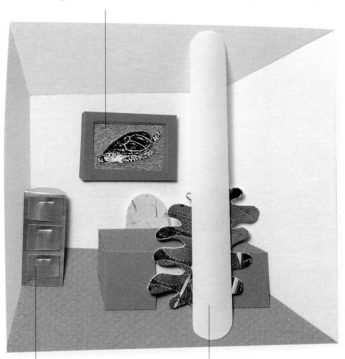

Put a steel filing cabinet in a place that does not hurt you. Placed in a corner behind you, its edges send hidden arrows at your back – find another place for it.

A column facing you is simply too deadly. You can try to block its effect with a large plant, but wrapping mirrors round it is more effective.

GOOD FENG SHUI AT WORK

It is not a good idea to have exposed book shelves around. They represent knives cutting into you. Placed behind, they are even more deadly. Put doors on your book shelves or arrange your books so that they blend with the shelves.

Having the door behind you is extremely bad feng shui. It means that even people you trust will betray you. It is very harmful to career luck.

Be careful what you put on your desktop. Avoid items that are pointed and have their edges pointing at you. Flowers are excellent and so, too, are crystals and other good-fortune symbols. Place them according to the compass sectors of the desk itself. Thus, place the table lamp on the south part of the desk and any flowers on the east side.

Wear colors that make you strong and energetic. Check the calendar on pages 28–29 and find out the ruling element of your year, then plan your wardrobe to include colors that are good for you. Red is good for those who need fire, such as people born in a wood year at the height of winter. Winter wood needs the warmth of fire. Wear black and blue for water, green for wood, yellow and beige for earth, and white for metal.

DESK DIMENSIONS

There are auspicious and inauspicious dimensions in feng shui. Lucky desk dimensions can actually help you gain promotion. These dimensions are based on the feng shui ruler. Experience shows that the desk most conducive to excellent career luck is one that is 33 x 60 x 33 inches (84 x 152 x 84cm). The dimensions suggested are excellent for working people, but there is some room for variation.

Desk lengths can vary according to your job. The following sets of dimensions have been chosen to ensure you will make absolutely no errors. Vary between 57 and 61 inches (145 and 155cm), between 41 and 44 inches (104 and 112cm), and between 49 and 52 inches (124 and 132cm).

Those who find the height suggested uncomfortable can place a platform under the chair or under the desk itself. Feng shui dimensions can also be applied to cabinets, cupboards, doors, and windows. Carpenters in Hong Kong, Singapore, and Malaysia all possess the feng shui ruler, which has to date been available only in Chinese, to make certain that the furniture they make conforms to the correct feng shui specifications.

There are also inauspicious dimensions, which create problems associated with stress, illness, and tension. Some of the inauspicious dimensions can also cause loss and betrayal. It is worth making an effort to adjust your office furniture to avoid these problems.

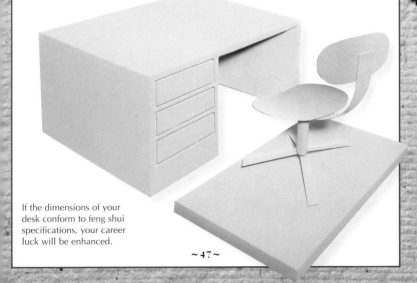

If the dimensions of your desk conform to feng shui specifications, your career luck will be enhanced.

FENG SHUI
FOR MANAGERS

NEGOTIATING DIRECTIONS

經理

Use the Kua formula directions to load the dice in your favor in every aspect of your work. Always carry a small compass and try to sit facing your best career direction when you are negotiating an important contract. It may not get you everything you want, but it will seriously increase your chances of getting a good deal. You can also use the same method when making a speech, negotiating your year-end bonus, or simply interviewing for a job.

negotiation
on the telephone

AUSPICIOUS TRAVEL DIRECTIONS

When planning your business trips – in fact, every time you travel in connection with work – try to plan your route and your calls to come from your auspicious direction. This applies to world travel by plane or local travel by car. Coming from your good direction means you are bringing luck with you!

With international travel, the direction you fly from depends entirely on the route you take. Thus, flying from the United States to Asia, you can travel eastward or westward. Check your directions carefully if the trip is an important one. This method should definitely be used if you are relocating for a few years.

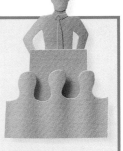

sales meetings   management meetings   training sessions

Each time you find yourself on a podium addressing an audience – at a sales convention, at a budget meeting, in a training session – try to orient your body so that you are facing your best career direction. This allows you to receive the auspicious energies in the room. Your audience will be very receptive and positive. The session will be a success.

At job interviews and office meetings, make it a habit to face your career direction when you speak. If this is not possible, at least face one of your four good directions.

interviews   divisional meetings

Always sit facing your best direction when you negotiate. Make it a habit until it becomes second nature. Be extra careful that you are not facing any of your inauspicious directions

IMPROVING THE BOTTOM LINE

Those who work in sales or marketing or have profit responsibility – sales people, branch officers, or insurance agents – can use feng shui to improve turnover and profits. This can be done through feng shui methods that address prosperity luck.

ENERGIZING THE
UNIVERSAL WEALTH SECTOR

The universal prosperity corner is the southeast of any room, office, or retail establishment and energizing this sector of the room attracts good fortune chi for the business or company. Place a plant in the southeast corner of your office or store. Make it a beautiful healthy plant, not one that looks half dead – and make sure it stays healthy. If it starts to get sickly, remove the yellowing or dead leaves and, if necessary, replace it altogether. Fake plants made of silk will be equally effective, but do not allow dried plants or flowers in the southeast whatever happens.

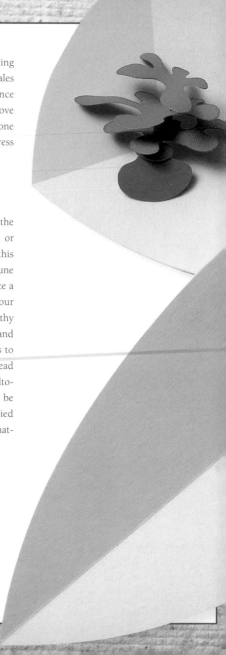

Plants and water features enhance good career luck when placed in the prosperity corner of the company or business.

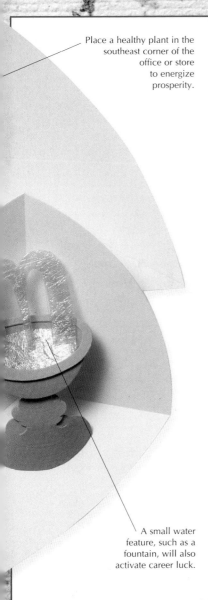

Place a healthy plant in the southeast corner of the office or store to energize prosperity.

A small water feature, such as a fountain, will also activate career luck.

ACTIVATING THE ORDER BOOK

An extremely useful feng shui tip that managers of retail branch establishments can use is to activate the order or sales book. This involves the use of three old Chinese coins. These coins have a small, square hole in the center. The square and the circular shapes together represent the harmonious unity of heaven and earth. Place the three coins, yang side up (the side with four characters is yang, while the side with two characters is yin), then tie the three coins together in any shape you like with thick red thread. The red thread is important as this energizes the flow of chi. Stick the coins on top of your order book. This method increases turnover and is an especially useful tip for sales people.

The three coins with red thread method can be used just as effectively with important files. Customer files, for example, can be activated in this way. These coins can also be hung above the main door on the inside. Get these coins (they are very inexpensive) from your local Chinese supermarket.

THE TIME DIMENSION

USING FLYING STAR FENG SHUI

時間

This type of feng shui addresses the changes of feng shui over time. This popular method is widely used in Hong Kong, Malaysia, and Singapore. The time aspects of this feng shui complement the space dimension of other feng shui methods. Flying star thus adds the vital dynamics of time

changes. This is a very advanced method and it is not really necessary for amateur practitioners to get too involved in its technical details. However, it is useful to have a reference table to enable you to investigate the impact of flying star on your own feng shui, particularly since this method is excellent for warning against the flying stars that bring serious bad luck. Being forewarned is often a great way of avoiding bad luck.

WHAT ARE THE FLYING STARS?

The stars refer to the numbers one to nine placed around a nine-sector grid, known as the Lo Shu magic square. The numbers around the grid fly – they change over time. The way they do this forms the crux of this method of feng shui.

Every day, month, and year, and every 20-year period has its own arrangement of numbers around the square. Every number has its own meanings and tells the feng shui expert who knows how to interpret the numbers, a great many things. To be forewarned, it is sufficient to monitor the period and year stars.

SOUTH

4	9	2
3	5	7
8	1	6

THE PERIOD OF SEVEN

We are currently living through the period of seven, which started in 1984 and does not end until the year 2003. This means that during this period, the number seven is deemed to be very lucky. The Lo Shu square for this period is shown here. Through an interpretation of the numbers, it describes the fortunate and less fortunate sectors up to the year 2003.

SOUTH

6	2	4
5	7	9
1	3	8

The original nine-sector Lo Shu square has the number five in the center. The numbers have been arranged so that the sum of any three numbers, taken vertically, horizontally or diagonally, is 15. In flying star feng shui, the numbers move from grid to grid and are interpreted according to which of them is in which square. Each of the eight sectors on the outside of the square represents a corner of the home. For analysis, the center is the ninth sector. South is placed at the top according to tradition, for presentation purposes only. Use a compass to identify the actual corners of your home.

During the period of seven, the bad-luck star number five is located in the east. This is interpreted to mean that if the main door of your home is located in the east, you should be very careful during this 20-year period. It also means that those sleeping in bedrooms located in the east should also be extra careful against being stabbed in the back.

The analysis will be more accurate when investigation is also conducted on the star numerals during the month and the year in question. When two or all three star numerals are fives in the same sector, loss due to extreme bad luck is certain during that month and year for anyone whose bedroom is in the sector where the fives occur together! When you become aware of the time when you need to be extra careful, one way of countering the bad luck is to travel away from home. Go for a vacation during that period, thereby avoiding the bad luck.

Year	Star numeral 2 is in the	Star numeral 5 is in the
1997	Southeast	West
1998	Center	Northeast
1999	Northwest	South
2000	West	North
2001	Northeast	Southwest
2002	South	East
2003	North	Southeast
2004	Southwest	Center
2005	East	Northwest
2006	Southeast	West

Year	Month 1	Month 2	Month 3	Month 4	Month 5
1997	Southwest	East Northwest	Southeast West	Northeast	South Northwest
1998	Northeast	Northwest South	West North	Northeast Southwest	South East
1999	Northeast Southwest	South East	North Southeast	Southwest	East Northwest
2000	Southwest	East Northwest	Southeast West	Northeast	Northwest South
2001	Northeast	Northwest South	West North	Northeast Southwest	South East

ROOMS TO AVOID
DURING SPECIFIC PERIODS
The yearly reference table
(*based on the lunar year)

The table opposite shows where the star five and star two occur together. The star two combined with five makes it extra dangerous. The two stars will also bring illness.

THE MONTHLY REFERENCE TABLES
(*based on the lunar months)

The table below indicates the dangerous sectors during each of the 12 lunar months over the next five years. These are the sectors where the star

Based on the reference table, left, rooms in the south are prone to illness in 1999. In 2002 rooms in the south and east should be avoided, and in 2005 rooms in the east should be avoided.

numerals two and five are located during that month. In the years 1998 and 2001 there are 13 months, so one of the months has been doubled.

Match where the star numerals two and five fall during the months indicated with those of the annual star numerals and the 20-year period star numerals.

Where twos and fives occur together is when that sector becomes dangerous and anyone occupying a room in an afflicted sector would do well to leave it for that time. Be particularly careful when the star numerals two and five fall into the east sector. This is because this is the sector afflicted with the five in the 20-year period flying star. The danger months and the directions are marked. When there are two dots, it means that both the sectors indicated are dangerous.

Month 6	Month 7	Month 8	Month 9	Month 10	Month 11	Month 12
West North	Northeast Southwest	South East	North Southeast	Southwest	East Northwest	Southeast West
South East	North Southeast	Southwest	East Northwest	Southeast West	Northeast	Northwest South
Southeast West	Northeast	Northwest South	West North	Northeast Southwest	South East	North Southeast
West North	Northeast Southwest	South East	North Southeast	Southwest	East Northwest	Southeast West
North Southeast	Southwest	East Northwest	Southeast West	Northeast	Northwest South	West North

INDEX

FURTHER READING

Kwok, Man-Ho and O'Brien, Joanne, *The Elements of Feng Shui,* ELEMENT BOOKS, SHAFTESBURY, 1991

Lo, Raymond *Feng Shui: The Pillars of Destiny (Understanding Your Fate and Fortune),* TIMES EDITIONS, SINGAPORE, 1995

Skinner, Stephen, *Living Earth Manual of Feng Shui: Chinese Geomancy,* PENGUIN, 1989

Too, Lillian *Chinese Astrology for Romance and Relationships,* KONSEP BOOKS, KUALA LUMPUR, 1996

Too, Lillian *Basic Feng Shui,* KONSEP BOOKS, KUALA LUMPUR, 1997

Too, Lillian *Dragon Magic,* KONSEP BOOKS, KUALA LUMPUR, 1996

Too, Lillian, *The Complete Illustrated Guide to Feng Shui,* ELEMENT BOOKS, SHAFTESBURY, 1996

Too, Lillian *Chinese Numerology in Feng Shui,* KONSEP BOOKS, KUALA LUMPUR, 1994

Too, Lillian *Feng Shui,* KONSEP BOOKS, KUALA LUMPUR, 1993

Too, Lillian *Practical Applications for Feng Shui,* KONSEP BOOKS, KUALA LUMPUR, 1994

Too, Lillian *Water Feng Shui for Wealth,* KONSEP BOOKS, KUALA LUMPUR, 1995

Walters, Derek *Feng Shui Handbook: A Practical Guide to Chinese Geomancy and Environmental Harmony,* AQUARIAN PRESS, 1991

USEFUL ADDRESSES

Feng Shui Design Studio
PO Box 705, Glebe, Sydney, NSW 2037,
Australia, Tel: 61 2 315 8258

Feng Shui Society of Australia
PO Box 1565, Rozelle, Sydney
NSW 2039, Australia

The Geomancer
The Feng Shui Store
PO Box 250, Woking, Surrey GU21 1YJ
Tel: 44 1483 839898
Fax: 44 1483 488998

Feng Shui Association
31 Woburn Place, Brighton BN1 9GA,
Tel/Fax: 44 1273 693844

Feng Shui Network International
PO Box 2133, London W1A 1RL,
Tel: 44 171 935 8935,
Fax: 44 171 935 9295

The School of Feng Shui
34 Banbury Road, Ettington,
Stratford-upon-Avon, Warwickshire
CV37 7SU. Tel/Fax: 44 1789 740116

The Feng Shui Institute of America
PO Box 488, Wabasso, FL 32970,
Tel: 1 407 589 9900 Fax: 1 407 589 1611

Feng Shui Warehouse
PO Box 3005, San Diego, CA 92163,
Tel: 1 800 399 1599 Fax: 1 800 997 9831

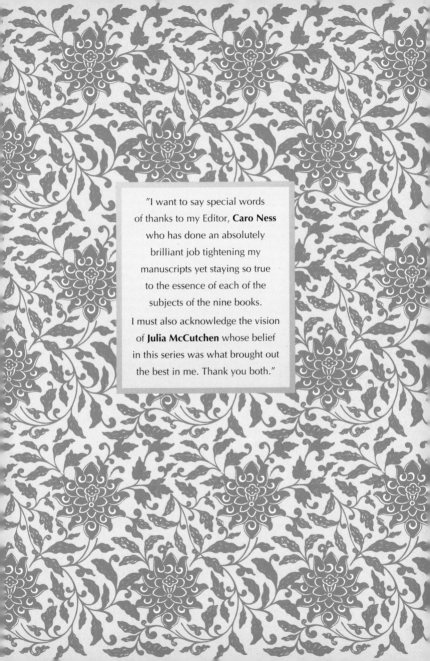

"I want to say special words
of thanks to my Editor, **Caro Ness**
who has done an absolutely
brilliant job tightening my
manuscripts yet staying so true
to the essence of each of the
subjects of the nine books.

I must also acknowledge the vision
of **Julia McCutchen** whose belief
in this series was what brought out
the best in me. Thank you both."

**Other titles in the
Feng Shui Fundamentals
series are:**

Children
Education
Eight Easy Lessons
Fame
Health
Love
Networking
Wealth